A New True Book

SKYLAB

By Dennis B. Fradin

*Photographs from The National Aeronautics
and Space Administration*

 CHILDRENS PRESS, CHICAGO

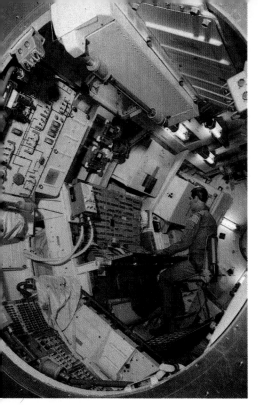

Interior view of the Skylab multiple docking adapter (MDA)
trainer used to train astronauts on earth for their space
journey. A dummy sits at the Apollo telescope mount controls.

Library of Congress Cataloging in Publication Data

Fradin, Dennis B.
  Skylab.

  (A New true book)
  Includes index.
  Summary: Describes the United States's first space
station and discusses its purpose and history.
  1. Skylab Program—Juvenile literature. [1. Skylab
Program] I. Title.
TL789.8.U6S5554   1984   629.44′5   83-23180
ISBN 0-516-01727-6

TABLE OF CONTENTS

What Was Skylab?... 5

Skylab's Three Goals... 11

Trouble!... 15

The "Fix-it Crew" to the Rescue... 17

The Three Crews... 20

People Can Live in Space!... 23

The Sun and the Earth... 39

The End of Skylab, the Future of Space Travel... 43

Words You Should Know... 46

Index... 47

Skylab space station. The Amazon River Valley
of Brazil can be seen in the background.

WHAT WAS SKYLAB?

A space station is a place on which people can live and work for long periods of time. On May 14, 1973, the United States launched its first space station. It was called Skylab. Ten minutes after lift-off Skylab was in orbit 270 miles above the earth. No people were aboard Skylab yet. The first crew was scheduled to rocket

up to Skylab the next
day—May 15.

The two little words in
Skylab—*sky* and *lab*—
explain what the space
station was. Skylab was a
laboratory sent up very
high into the sky.

The main part of the
118-foot-long Skylab was
the orbital workshop. This
was where the crews
would live. The orbital
workshop was like an
apartment in space. It had

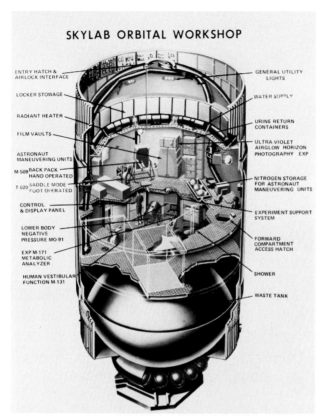

SKYLAB ORBITAL WORKSHOP

ENTRY HATCH &
AIRLOCK INTERFACE

LOCKER STOWAGE

RADIANT HEATER

FILM VAULTS

ASTRONAUT
MANEUVERING UNITS

M-509 BACK PACK
HAND OPERATED

T-020 SADDLE MODE
FOOT OPERATED

CONTROL
& DISPLAY PANEL

LOWER BODY
NEGATIVE
PRESSURE MO-91

EXP M-171
METABOLIC
ANALYZER

HUMAN VESTIBULAR
FUNCTION M-131

GENERAL UTILITY
LIGHTS

WATER SUPPLY

URINE RETURN
CONTAINERS

ULTRA VIOLET
AIRGLOW HORIZON
PHOTOGRAPHY EXP

NITROGEN STORAGE
FOR ASTRONAUT
MANEUVERING UNITS

EXPERIMENT SUPPORT
SYSTEM

FORWARD
COMPARTMENT
ACCESS HATCH

SHOWER

WASTE TANK

Cutaway view of
the Skylab's orbital
workshop (OWS),
one of the
five parts of
the space station.

an area for sleeping. It had
food freezers and a table
for eating. It had a
bathroom. There was also
a room where the astronauts
would perform experiments.

Much of Skylab's equipment was on its outside. There were eight telescopes for studying the sun. There was a shield that lay over Skylab like a roof. The shield would protect Skylab from meteoroids and also shade it from the sun. In addition, Skylab had six solar power wings. Four of the wings looked like the blades on a windmill. The other two looked like the wings on

Official emblem
of the
Skylab program

an old airplane. These six
wings were very important.
They contained devices to
convert the sun's energy
into electricity for Skylab.

Another important part of
Skylab was the multiple

Above: Multiple docking adapter (MDA)
Right: Astronaut Edward G. Gibson
photographed outside Skylab.

docking adapter. When astronauts rocketed up to Skylab, they would park their *Apollo* rocket at the multiple docking adapter. Then they would enter Skylab through a special air lock.

SKYLAB'S THREE GOALS

Skylab had three main goals. First, scientists wondered if people could live in space for long periods of time. Between 1969 and 1972 the U.S. had landed astronauts on the moon six times. The moon trips had been just a few days each. Trips to distant planets would take months or even years. Could people live in space

Astronaut Alan L. Bean records information in the orbital workshop while holding on to tape that floats free in the zero gravity of space.

for that long? The Skylab astronauts would help answer that question.

Skylab's second goal was to study the sun—the star that gives the earth heat and light. From earth we can't see everything

Astronaut Paul J. Weitz sits at the controls of the Apollo telescope mount located in the multiple docking adapter (MDA).

that occurs on the sun because the earth's atmosphere blocks out some of the sun's rays. From space, Skylab's telescopes were expected to reveal new information about the sun.

Skylab 1 space station cluster photographed against the earth.

Skylab's third goal was to study the earth. From 270 miles up, astronauts could see and photograph many features on earth that couldn't be spotted from the ground.

TROUBLE!

As Skylab headed into orbit, trouble struck. The shield that protected Skylab from meteoroids and the sun's heat ripped away. Without this shield, temperatures inside Skylab soared past 120 degrees Fahrenheit. Astronauts couldn't live in that heat. Also, one of the solar power wings was ripped off and another didn't go into place. This meant that Skylab was without much of its electric power.

The May 15 trip to Skylab was postponed. Meanwhile, scientists tried to think of ways to cool Skylab and provide it with more electricity. If that couldn't be done, the $2.5 billion Skylab would be nothing more than a heap of space junk.

THE "FIX-IT CREW" TO THE RESCUE

On May 25—ten days late—the first crew blasted off. The crew, Charles Conrad, Jr., Dr. Joseph P.

Close-up of the Skylab's command service module

Astronauts Charles Conrad, Jr., (background) and Joseph P.
Kerwin (foreground) fixed Skylab's damaged solar power wings.

Kerwin, and Paul J. Weitz, carried materials to repair Skylab. As they chased Skylab in their *Apollo* spacecraft, Conrad told scientists on the ground: "We can fix anything!"

Conrad was right. The "Fix-it Crew" put an awning over Skylab to protect it from the sun's heat. They pulled the solar power wing into place. Skylab was now ready for people to live on it.

THE THREE CREWS

Over a nine-month period, three separate crews rocketed up to live and work on Skylab. Each crew had three men. One was the commander, the person in charge. The second was the science pilot, who knew a lot about the experiments and scientific equipment. The third was the pilot, the expert on space flight.

Here are the three
Skylab crews and the
dates they spent aboard
the space station:

Crew One, the "Fix-it Crew" (28 days in space, from
May 25, 1973 to June 22, 1973).
Commander: Charles Conrad, Jr. (center)
Science pilot: Dr. Joseph P. Kerwin (left)
Pilot: Paul J. Weitz (right)

Crew Two (59 days in space, from July 28, 1973
to September 25, 1973)
Commander: Alan L. Bean (right)
Science pilot: Dr. Owen K. Garriott (left)
Pilot: Jack R. Lousma (center)

Crew Three (84 days in space, from November 16,
1973 to February 8, 1974)
Commander: Gerald P. Carr (left)
Science Pilot: Dr. Edward G. Gibson (center)
Pilot: William R. Pogue (right)

PEOPLE CAN LIVE IN SPACE!

Imagine orbiting earth once every ninety-three minutes and zooming through space at more than seventeen thousand miles per hour! That's what the Skylab astronauts did. Yet they ate, slept, and did most of the things people do on earth—with one big difference.

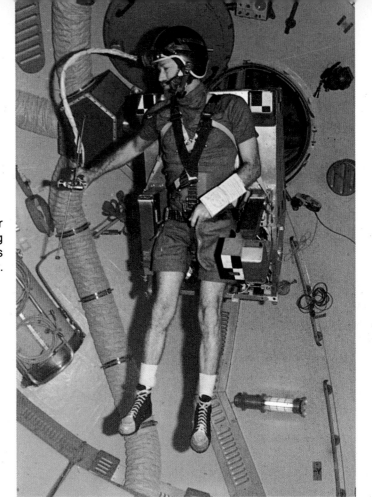

Astronaut Gerald P. Carr tests maneuvering equipment in Skylab's zero gravity.

The difference was gravity, the force that holds us down to earth. Planets, stars, and other heavenly bodies have gravity.

However, Skylab was so high above the earth and moving so fast that gravity did not hold the men to the floor of the ship.

Zero gravity, as it's called, was fun. The astronauts could float like bubbles throughout the spaceship. They hung upside down like bats. They balanced upside down on each other's fingertips.

To work outside Skylab
the astronauts had to
wear space suits.
The ward room (below left)
and the waste management
compartment (below right)
were designed to deal
with the problems
the astronauts would
have working in
zero gravity.

Zero gravity also poses problems. Imagine trying to eat peas or roast beef with the food flying all over the place. Imagine floating off the bed in your sleep. Imagine trying to take a shower. The astronauts had special devices to help them do these everyday tasks without much trouble.

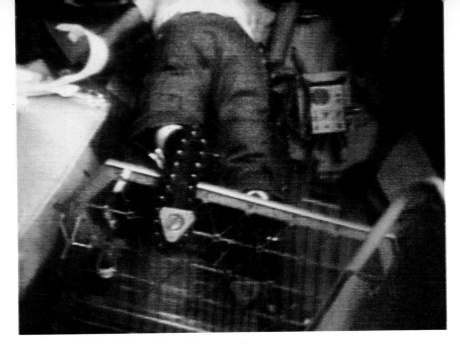

Close-up of the triangular plates on the astronaut's shoes. These plates fitted into the grid floor and held the astronaut in place.

The astronauts wore special shoes. The shoes had cleats that fitted into holes on Skylab's floor. These special shoes helped the astronauts stand in one place without floating away.

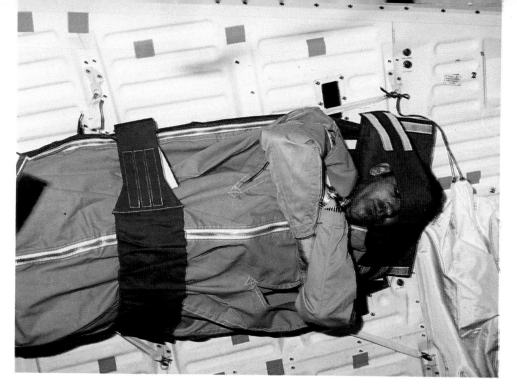
A sleeping bag and belts hold this sleeping astronaut in place.

The astronauts slept in
sleeping bags that hung
from the ceiling. Once they
had zipped themselves up
in the bags, they didn't
have to worry about
floating off in their sleep.

The astronauts ate
cereal, beef, vegetables,
and many other foods.
They took the food out of
freezers and heated it on
trays. Magnets held down
their knives, forks, and
spoons. Plastic covers kept
the food from floating
away. The astronauts drank
water and other liquids
from plastic bottles much
like baby bottles.

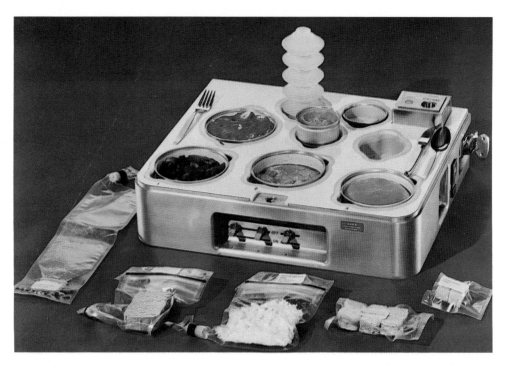

Close-up of the food tray (above) and astronaut Jack R. Lousma eating in space.

When the astronauts went to the bathroom, an air blower aimed the wastes into the proper place. To shower, they climbed into a device that looked like an old washing machine. A special hose sucked up the water drops that drifted around after the shower.

To keep their hearts and other muscles fit, the Skylab crews exercised. This was very important. In

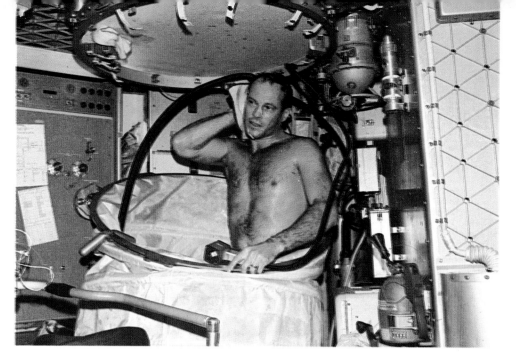

Jack R. Lousma (above) takes a hot bath. The curtain is pulled up from the floor and attached to the ceiling. The water is drawn off by a vacuum system before the curtain is opened again. To exercise their leg and back muscles, the astronauts worked out on this treadmill (below). The cords, connected to a harness worn by the astronauts, supply the necessary downward pressure.

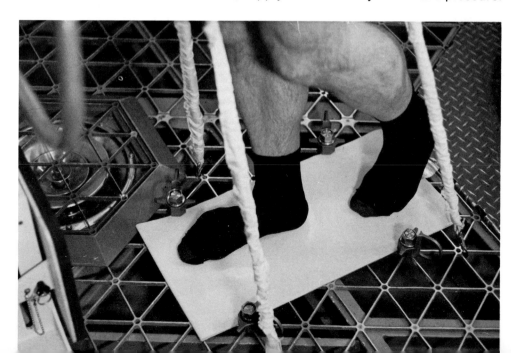

space muscles don't have to fight gravity to do their work. As a result they tend to weaken. The danger comes when space travelers return to earth. It may be difficult for their hearts and other muscles to handle the bigger work load that gravity creates.

Crew One exercised a half hour each day. They returned to earth in pretty good shape. Crew Two exercised an hour per day.

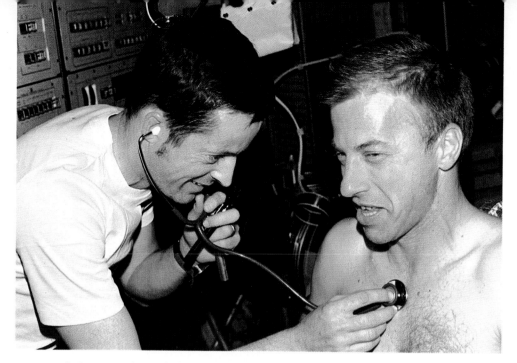

Astronaut Joseph P. Kerwin, M.D. checks the heart rate of Paul J. Weitz.

That helped them spend more time in space and return home in better condition. The third crew exercised an hour and a half each day. They set records for space travel— spending eighty-four days

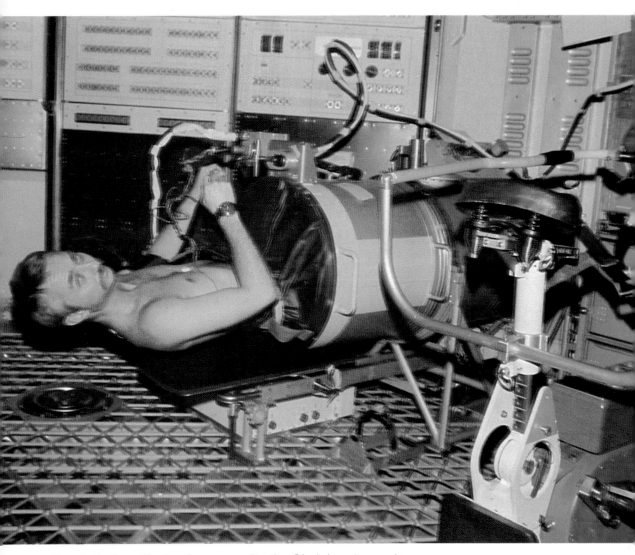

To study the effects of zero gravity the Skylab astronauts
took part in a number of medical and scientific experiments.
The equipment Astronaut Owen K. Garriott is using provided
information about the human body's adaptation to living without
the pull of gravity.

in space, circling earth 1,214 times, traveling 34.5 million miles—yet returned in the best shape of all.

Medical tests kept track of the astronauts' health. It was found that after about forty days in space, the human body adjusts to zero gravity. This means that future astronauts should be able to spend many months on space voyages.

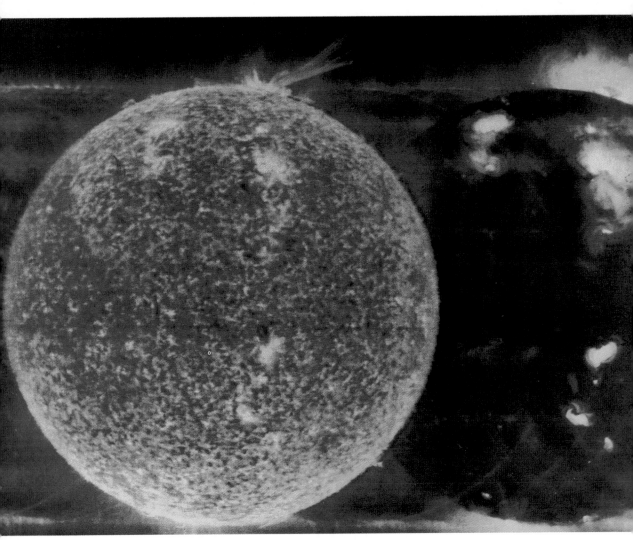

Skylab's telescope captured this picture of a solar eruption.

THE SUN AND EARTH

The three Skylab missions took more than 160,000 pictures of the sun. From these it was learned that the sun is more complex and more violent than had been thought. For example, many solar flares were seen. Solar flares are huge bursts of energy from a small area of the sun.

Above: Himalaya Range in Asia.
Below right: Clouds cover the Pacific Ocean west of Baja, California.
Below: Portion of South Island, New Zealand, at left is the
Tasman Sea; Cape Foulwind is at the upper left.

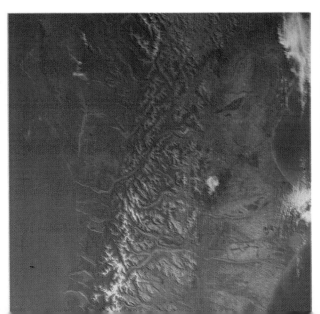

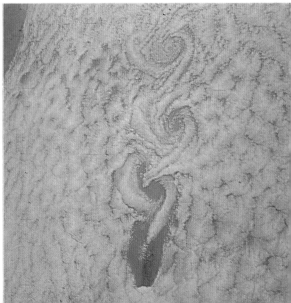

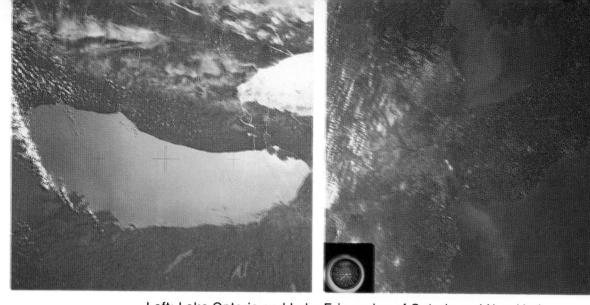

Left: Lake Ontario and Lake Erie region of Ontario and New York.
Right: The metropolitan area of Detroit, Michigan. The 25-mile-long
Detroit River separates the city from Windsor, Ontario, Canada.

New information was
also learned about the
earth. The thousands of
photographs taken of our
planet showed much about
its weather and oceans. Oil
and mineral deposits were
spotted. So were signs of
air and water pollution.

The Skylab crews returned
to earth in their command
module. After re-entry
into the earth's atmosphere
parachutes (right) were used
to slow the spacecraft's
descent. When it splashed
down in the Pacific Ocean,
navy swimmers placed a
collar around it and hoisted
the command module aboard
a nearby recovery ship.

THE END OF SKYLAB, THE FUTURE OF SPACE TRAVEL

On February 8, 1974, the third Skylab crew packed up and reentered the little *Apollo* spacecraft. They left Skylab and rocketed home to earth. They splashed down near San Diego, California, and were soon plucked from the ocean.

Although its passengers were gone, Skylab still orbited the earth. It did so for more than five years. Then on July 12, 1979, it fell from the sky. A few pieces of Skylab landed on Australia. The rest of Skylab probably plunged into the ocean.

One day, people will travel to the planets and beyond. Those future space

travelers should remember
the Skylab space station. It
taught us that people can
live in space.

WORDS YOU SHOULD KNOW

Apollo spacecraft(uh • POL • oh SPAISS • kraft) — the small spacecraft that carried the astronauts up to Skylab and later returned them to earth

astronauts(AST • roh • nautz) — space explorers

commander(kuh • MAN • der) — the person in charge of Skylab when it was in orbit

earth(ERTH) — the planet on which we live

electricity(ih • lek • TRISS • itee) — a kind of energy that provides us with heat, light, and power

gravity(GRAV • ih • tee) — the force that holds us down to earth

laboratory(LAB • rah • tor • ee) — a place where experiments are done

meteoroids(ME • tee • or • oidz) — particles of stone or metal in the solar system

multiple docking adapter(MUL • tih • pil DAH • king ah • DAP • ter) — the place where the astronauts parked their *Apollo* spacecraft after rocketing up to Skylab

orbit(OR • bit) — the path an object takes when it moves around another object

orbital workshop — the area of Skylab where the astronauts lived and worked

pilot(PIE • lit) — the member of Skylab's crew who was an expert on space flight

science pilot(SYE • ence) — the member of Skylab's crew who knew a lot about the experiments and scientific equipment

Skylab(SKY • lab) — a space station launched by the United States in 1973

solar(SO • ler) — relating to the sun

solar flare(SO • ler FLAIR) — a great outburst of energy from a small area of the sun

solar power wings(SO • ler POW • er WINGZ) — wings that contained devices to convert the sun's energy into electricity for Skylab

space station(SPAISS STAY • shun) — an artificial satellite large enough so that people can live and work on it

sun — the star which, because it is the closest one to earth, gives us heat and light

telescopes(TEL • eh • scohpz) — instruments that make distant objects look closer

zero gravity(ZEE • roh GRAV • ih • tee) — a condition in which there is no gravity

INDEX

air lock, 10

Apollo spacecraft, 10, 19, 43

Australia, 44

bathroom, 7, 32

Bean, Alan L., 22

Carr, Gerald P., 22

commander, crew, 20

Conrad, Charles, Jr., 17, 19, 21

Crew One, 5, 17, 19, 21, 34

Crew Two, 22, 34

Crew Three, 22, 35, 43

earth, study of, 14, 41

eating, 7, 27, 30

electric power, 9, 15

exercise, 32, 34, 35

experiments, 7, 20

"Fix-it Crew," 17, 19

food, 27, 30

Garriott, Owen K., 22

Gibson, Edward G., 22

goals, of Skylab, 11-14

gravity, 24, 25, 27, 34, 37

Kerwin, Joseph P., 17, 19, 21

Lousma, Jack R., 22

meteoroids, 8, 15

moon, astronauts on, 11

multiple docking adapter, 9, 10

orbit, of Skylab, 5, 23, 44

orbital workshop, 6, 7

pilot, 20

planets, trips to, 11

Pogue, William R., 22

San Diego, California, 43

science pilot, 20

shield, over Skylab, 8, 15

shoes, 28

shower, 27, 32

Skylab, definition of word, 6

sleeping, 7, 27, 29
solar flares, 39
solar power wings, 8, 9, 16, 19
space, living in, 11, 12
speed, of Skylab, 23

sun, study of, 8, 12, 13, 39
telescopes, 8, 13
Weitz, Paul J., 19, 21
wings, solar power, 8, 9, 16, 19
zero gravity, 25, 27, 37

About the Author

Dennis Fradin attended Northwestern University on a partial creative writing scholarship and graduated in 1967. He has published stories and articles in such places as Ingenue, The Saturday Evening Post, Scholastic, Chicago, Oui, *and* National Humane Review. *His previous books include the Young People's Stories of Our States series for Childrens Press, and* Bad Luck Tony *for Prentice-Hall. In the True book series Dennis has written about astronomy, farming, comets, archaeology, movies, and the space lab. He is married and the father of three children.*